GRUMPY CAT
COLORING BOOK

Dover Publications, Inc.
Mineola, New York

Grumpy Cat™

Grumpy Cat and Related Artwork © and ® Grumpy Cat Limited
www.GrumpyCats.com Used Under License

Illustrations by David Cutting

Bibliographical Note

Grumpy Cat Coloring Book is a new work, first published by Dover Publications, Inc., in 2014. Grumpy Cat™ and related artwork used by permission of Grumpy Cat Limited.

International Standard Book Number

ISBN-13: 978-0-486-79163-0
ISBN-10: 0-486-79163-7

Manufactured in the United States by Courier Corporation
79163703   2015
www.doverpublications.com

This is my coloring book.
Do you like to color? I DON'T CARE.

GRUMPIN' AROUND THE WORLD:

Russian: NYET!

So I made a list of things I like. Yes, this is a blank page.

Met a leprechaun once... It was delicious.

Grumps of the Silver Screen:
GRUMPY

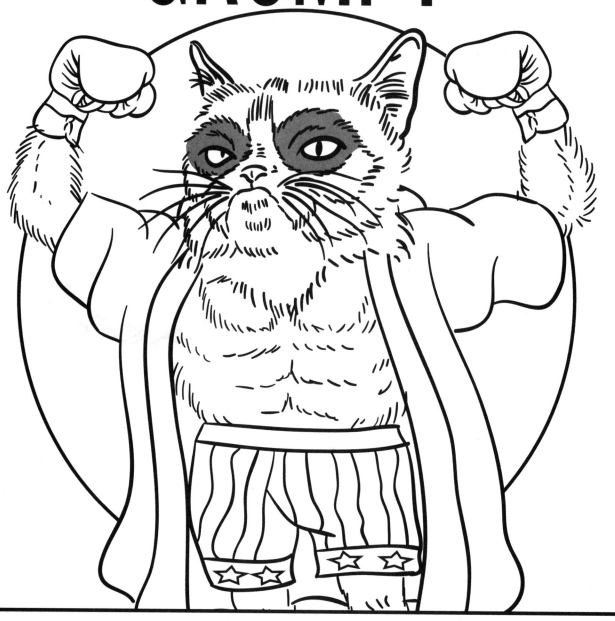

Get me out of here!

**Feliz Navi
DON'T**

GRUMPY ON THE GO

GRUMPIN' AROUND THE WORLD:

Japanese: IIE!

Grumps of the Silver Screen:

THE FUTURE IS AWFUL.

The TermiNOtor

Valentine's Day – NO.

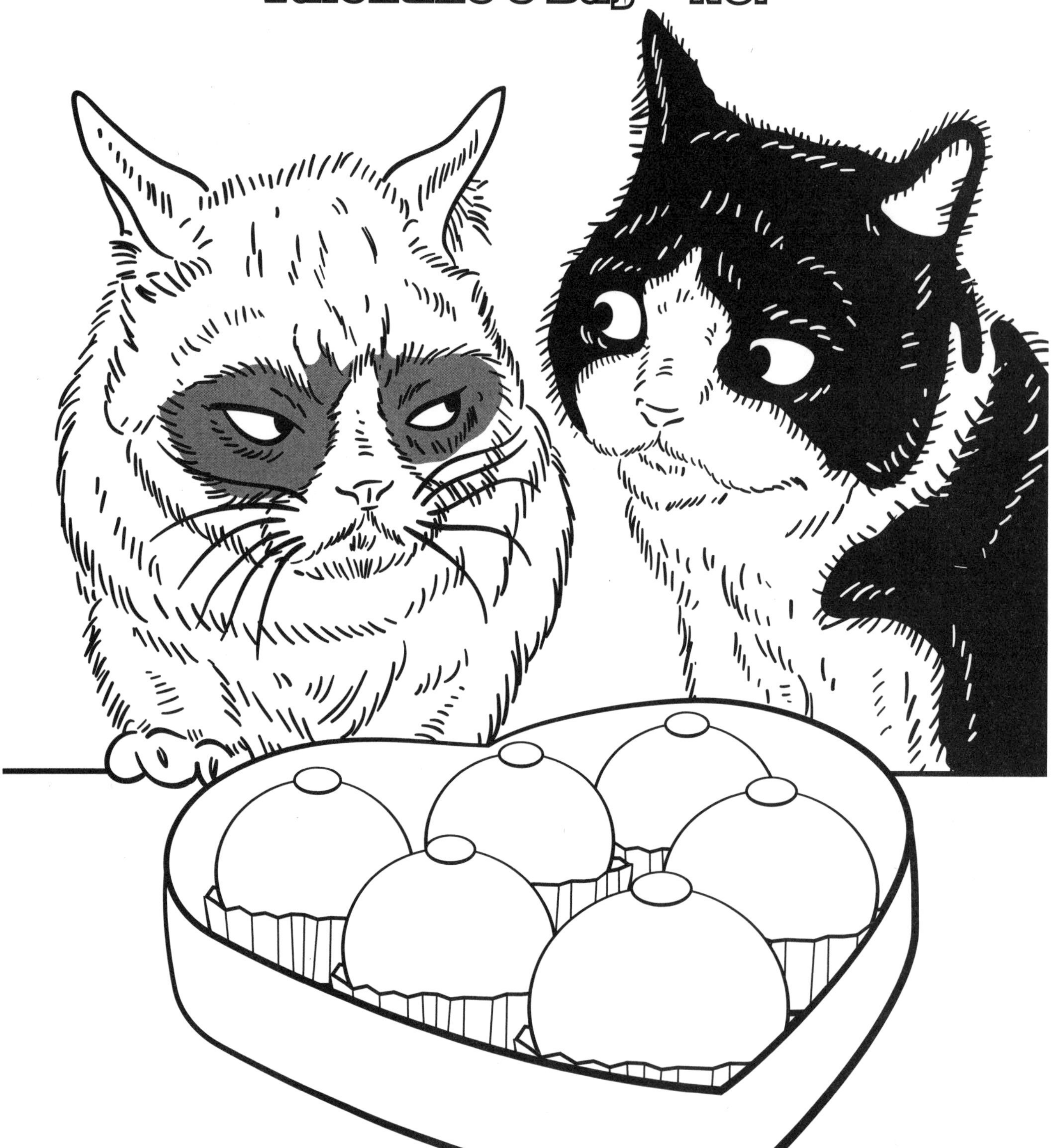

If you're happy and you know it... Go Away.

GRUMPIN' AROUND THE WORLD:

Spanish: ¡NO!

Spring is in the air... It's miserable

AbracadabNO

Grumps of the Silver Screen:
The Wizard of No

Santa left me coal. GOOD.

GRUMPY ON THE GO

The uNOcycle

GRUMPIN' AROUND THE WORLD:

Portuguese: NÃO

Grumps of the Silver Screen:
Indiana No

and the
Raiders
of the
GET LOST ARK

No. I'm still not impressed.

Click to share... NO!

MY FAVORITE WORDS:

NO.

This list is over.

GOOD.

(Okay, that's two!)

I went to a tea party once...
IT WAS AWFUL

GRUMPIN' AROUND THE WORLD:

Hindi: NAHIN!

Grumps of the Silver Screen:
Doctor NO

"Romeo and Juliet" is a great story. It's so sad.

GRUMPY ON THE GO

Row Row Row Your NO!

They say it takes more muscles in your face to frown rather than smile. What can I say? I'm addicted to fitness.

Black is the new black

GRUMPY ON THE GO

Demolishing happiness